T0159222

I'm A Warrior
For Jesus

WelLiBelLiE KiDs BoOks

Emmazina Day

authorHOUSE®

AuthorHouse™
1663 Liberty Drive
Bloomington, IN 47403
www.authorhouse.com
Phone: 1 (800) 839-8640

Published by AuthorHouse   09/19/2017

ISBN: 978-1-4772-1153-3 (sc)
ISBN: 978-1-4772-1154-0 (e)

Library of Congress Control Number: 2012909198

Print information available on the last page.

Any people depicted in stock imagery provided by Thinkstock are models, and such images are being used for illustrative purposes only. Certain stock imagery © Thinkstock.

This book is printed on acid-free paper.

CONTENTS

God grant me the serenity to accept the things I cannot change

The courage to change the things I can. And
the wisdom to know the different

(King James version)

DEDICATION

I would like to dedicate, this Book to my first Love. My savior Jesus Christ. I give thanks with all of my being without him I am nothing. I would like to thank my family, for their support. For being understanding. While writing this little book. To my Mother, grandmother who has passed on. Who have always encourage me, by saying, that I can do anything. All I had to do was to put my mind to it. To all my family members who said we love you. Keep writing.

Thank you! family. For being there at the right time.
For me, So many blessing and lessons learned.

God, family and love. Will always Be forever.

DR. JESUS

What a beautiful name! What a powerful name Jesus! What a name we all should know the name is Dr. Jesus! Can anyone think of a time when you needed Jesus. When Jesus, was not there for you. He's always in the midst of all things. I promise you he's there for you. Pray and ask your heavenly father whatever you need from him. Take it all to Jesus… The bible tells us God die for our sins and he did. So I love to call Jesus name, Jesus sweet Jesus!... The bible tells us Jesus is coming back one day don't know when but he's coming. Just read the book of revelation.

Read the bible for yourself it's in there, just saying. Jesus is a jealous God, he loves for us all to pray to him. Call him and the morning call him in the evening there's no charge to ask or talk to Dr. Jesus. Don't turn Jesus away. You do not want your soul to be lost. Jesus can fix every problem and heal every pain. Come on let's bless his name. Just saying.

WHAT ABOUT YOU?

Yes you! God is so good to me! Yes sir! Take a moment. To reflect on all of your blessings that God, has bestowed upon us all. What about you? I would like to say, "Thank You, Jesus" for loving us all. And carrying me, as well as the whole world in his heart. We are so undeserving of God's love. But he loves us all. When I felt like there were so many obstacles in my life, I just remember to share what I've learned with others. The Lord promised that He will never leave us. God can do all things, nothing is too big or too small for God, just ask. Pray when you're feeling good about yourself. If there are no problems going on in your life. Still pray. Just believe in the Lord and have faith, Jesus is alive today and always. God, will never leave you, let's pray for peace and we should never forget to pray for guidance and encouragement. Remember the most high is the same today tomorrow and always just sayin...

Jesus, is always listening. Just sayin'...

The Lord is my light and my salvation whom shall I fear? The Lord is the stronghold of my life - of whom shall I be afraid?
Psalm 27:1

Forever Is My Word

Forever is my word... Love is a place where two lovers go. When true love takes over them both. Remember, keep God in your life. Will make any relationship a bless one. Love is for ever

ONE WINTER NIGHT

When Bella was a little girl, Late one night she awoke to
the warmth of her feet on the bedroom floor. Bella, said to
herself my feet feels so hot on this floor. Bella, little feet

Touch the floor on this cold winter night there was no carpet on
the floor. They were wood floors The floor was so warm to Bella's
feet almost to hot. But strangely enough just right, because her
feet was so cold. Bella, little feet was always very cold. Bella, was
headed to the bathroom. There was not a little night light for
her to see during her nightly visits, Bella, could see around the
room in the dark, she saw her own shadow. Outside her window
was a street light, that comes on every night at 7:00 sharp.

Bella has gotten up so many times before but this time it was different.
Something was wrong she felt danger she smelled smoke Bella, open
her bedroom door and knocked on her Mother's door she came to the
door she saw the smoke she said Bella,! run next door and knock on the
neighbor's door keep knocking until someone come to the door and tell
them to call for help!!! She did exactly as her mother ask her to do. With
no shoes on know coat on. It was freezing outside. This is an emergency
Bella, thought to herself. When she got outside she could see the
flames coming from the back of the house where she had just used the
restroom. Bella, started to pray Jesus help my family to safety. And safely
please. Do not let them burn in this old cold house. with the cold floors.
Bella was only four years old. When she saw the red flashing lights,

neighbors all around her came out their homes to help. Bella didn't see her Mom! she panic she started to call out Mommy!, Mommy!! The neighbor held, Bella, close to her giving her motherly love. Bella just wanted to run into her mother's arms. Bella's mom came out the burning house with her little brother and sister. It was such a joy for Bella, to see her family and to know they all are ok. Mother came and stood by Bella with her step Dad, when she heard mommy say where is my baby? Bella's step Dad took off running the man with the fire suite on said it's too late, no one can go back in the burning house, well my stepfather took off running and went back inside despite what he was told. What a courageous Dad! oh my goodness the fear we all had what seem like such a long time but it was only minutes... here comes Bella's stepdad with baby Lullabye, in his arms. Know one was injured

Thank you Jesus! What a joy to see her baby sister Lullibye, she is a beautiful baby girl she had no idea what was going on. How much danger she was in. God mercy and grace had saved Lullabye. Bella said a small prayer.

Thank you Jesus amen

Our heavenly Father, wants you to draw Close to him, God knows our circumstances he is closer than we think, we just need to keep praying to him, know matter what. Know matter how busy we think we are, make a little time for him. Jesus, died on the cross for all our sins. Only Jesus can bring you peace.

BROKEN HEARTED

Never stop living and loving life. Life is a gift from God. Never
stop loving yourself, be happy. Never allow someone else to destroy
your happiness or peace of mind. Learn to understand who you are,
learn the value of your self-worth. You are a beautiful person who
deserve the best! Never love someone more than you love yourself.
Falling in love is a beautiful thing. Sometimes people seem to forget,
how to love another person or how to treat the one they love.

Therefore, letting a third person in your life, or just fall out of love,
or just grow apart. Either way, whatever the case may be, heartaches
do exists. You have, to determine how much of a broken, heart you
want to deal with. Pull yourself up. UP! off the floor, hold your head
up high, brush yourself off, and think about what, makes you happy.
Afterwards, go live life. God said bring all your problems to him in
prayer. Please Keep looking forward and do not look back. The past
is just what it is, the past. life can be hard if you make it hard, on
yourself, take one step at a time, You cannot change anything, and
the pass. Nothing is easy in this life. You feel lost and sometimes
lonely time heals the brokenhearted. Well before you know it, you
have moved on in life, and ready to find love all over again. LOVE...
Falling in love is wonderful, and the feelings just flows between two.
The attraction is there. The chemistry of love is with you both. The true
meaning of real love, is GOD, having a broken heart can be painful,
you can not even think straight. Yes, you may hurt to the core of your
being and become heartless. Yes, you may not have any answers to

where your life is going, however, it's not the end of the world. You may feel this way for the moment. Please put God first, pray over your situation, and the Lord will heal your broken heart in time.

I'm Just sayin'...

Mother and Daughter's Love

A Mother's love, for her daughter. Is a love, you cannot describe. When a mother loves you, she loves you unconditionally, she's there for your every whim, every tear that falls. You can count on mother. To be there for her daughter. A daughter loves her Mother with so much love, she, respect her and she's proud to be her daughter. A daughter, is there to talk to mother as well, when she's older. A daughter can wipe away her tears, from her cheeks. With a loving smile she will I'm here mother.

A mother will take all your worries your frustrations, away by sitting you down for a nice home cook meal a cup of coffee, made just the way you like it. And listen to you with whatever you have on your mind.

Mother, will then look at you and say everything will be alright my daughter, with a smile only a mother can give, you hear her voice and you just know your be ok. Mother, is always called, Mom. Or mommy, There is know words to say, because Mom's will say whatever she feels her heart needs to say to her child whether it's right or wrong we listen to Mom. We do not follow her every advice, at times. We grow weak, when we stray away. Sometimes we do not listen to Mom, when she speaks knowledge into our hearts. Are we listening? Sometimes, we are and sometimes not. Some of us daughters act like we have all the answers and we do not. Not realizing how much of this knowledge she's trying to relay to us, is very important to our hearts and mind.

Until you're much older. Then we realize, Jesus says. honor your mother and your Father and your days shall be long upon the land.

A mother, is a strong women whose love, has no ending for her children. No matter what age, they may become. A mother can feed you, like she feeds her baby, Without having a bottle. Or having to wash a bottle. As you get older, she will still feed you with advice. She will never sugar coat the truth this is the way God, has made a women. A women with soft skin and soft hands. When she looks into your eyes. She means what she says. And she says what she means

Almighty God, knew exactly what he was doing, when he made a woman, called Mother. One thing we know we can not live on this earth, without a woman called Mother

Cherish your Mom always.

YOUR HEART AND MIND ARE

forever one.

Loving someone is like caring for a garden, love it too much or too little and it dies,but love it just right and it will live forever.

I will love you all my life and when I die I will still love you through eternity. I will always Love you. Just sayin...

LOOK AT ME

Who am I ? Look at me! What do you see

when you look at me? Look at me!

I am me! I am not you!

I feel, I hurt, I have pain but still I love.

Just like you! God made us both" to be different.

I'm me. and you're you.

Just sayin...

Jesus Said

Surely I am with you always,

to the very end of the age.

Matthew 28:20

When Love Hurts

When love hurts and you need to call on Jesus, do so my friend. When the pain of a heartache in the pit of your stomach hurt so deep and you just call on Jesus! to relieve the heartache. When love hurts, Things are not always the way you planned them to be. When love hurts People grow and you can grow apart as well. When love hurts you remember the good times, When love hurts when it's time to say good bye. When love hurts just talk to Jesus to ease the pain this too shall pass.

TO LOVE A FRIEND

It's impossible to find good friends. It's like finding a needle in a broomstick. When you do find a best friend, they live forever in your heart. True friends are so difficult, so impossible to let go. Best friends will stick by you no matter what, my ride and die

Friends are forever. Jesus, shows you their loyalty
their friendship and also show you their love.

Hold on to your best friends.

Hold on to your dear friends. full of laughs, always
keep a smile on your face they keep you happy. To
love a friend is to be a true friend. Just sayin'...

WHY YA'LL ?

Why do Love hurt?

why do we fall in love to get hurt?

Why do we listen to the BS? Ladies, ladies! and gentlemen,
guard your hearts. Relaxed and let go,of the hurt, be mindful
of your new found love. Love is and can be very beautiful we all
need that special someone in our lives, there is times Love can
hurt but wonderful at the same time as well. Just sayin...

DEAR FATHER

I come to you in prayer for guidance. I need you in my life always Jesus. I need you to help me father, to show me the right things to do before I turn to make, a wrong decision in this stressful world. Dear Jesus only you can take away the pain and stress of everyday living I endure in life. I come to you father and prayer when I'm in pain, I call on you. Father for all my needs. I need you to help me step by step, and the name of Jesus I pray

Amen

Matthew 6:33

Seek first God's kingdom and his righteousness, and
all these things will be given to you as well.

There is a place where your fingerprints still rest.

your kisses still linger, and your whisper still softly echos, in my ear. It's the place where a part of you will forever be a part of me your heart.

My Love my life. I've been waiting to say to you

You're my love, my world my everything

I Love You. I love you to the stars that shine so brightly in the sky to give us light to see each other love. I love you so much

my heart sing a song of happy beats, I'm So grateful Jesus sent you to me as a loving gift. I'm in love with you.

I've been holding on to my love just for you and only

YOU.

My Love

WHY COMPLAIN

Why? We have so many blessing to be thankful for. Just look around. God gave us the gift of life. The gift of our five senses, the gift to sing, to dance to love, Let's be thankful. To some people, they may think or say, some of us have more blessings than others be happy for what you been given do not show envy, or jealousy. God gave us all a very special "gift of life."

Enjoy what have. We want what God has for us. And we should, not think, about what God has done for others. Not with envy. Just know he can do the same for you as well. Therefore, be thankful, for what God can and will do for you. We all fall short of God's glory and he still blesses us, Almighty God has bestowed so much love to us all.

We must not take our blessings for granted for no one is perfect. Be thankful and don't complain.

why complain?

RECOGNIZE

We need to recognize love, when we see it! love comes
in all shapes and sizes. Why wait to let the other person
know. How much you really care? Grandmom!

We care we love you, family and friends listen! we all need to show
love to one another. Almighty God, blessed us to love and care for each
other. When someone we love is helpless or sick. We need to recognize,
and not wait until they are no longer with us. Or to say I love you.

But we are quick to say, ok well I'm going to call you but I forgot.
I just got so busy working and I just forgot. You may even say I got
so busy with the kids. Doing so many things. And I just forgot. I
just had no time to visit, there are so many excuses we use. Mother I
was so tired and I was going to stop by to see you. It's just been one
thing or another that's keeping me from visiting. We do not mean
any harm, we all just get caught up, and our own daily lives, so busy
we all are. We just forget at times, to take the time, out to say

I Love You. To the ones who means, the most to us. We wasn't to busy to say Mother or Grandma, can you, will you take me to the mall or drop me off to the movies whatever the reason is Grandma, Mother or Dad was always there with open arms a loving smile. she or he may say ok come on... let's go... you guys do not make any sense. But guess what Recognize. She took the time out for you! she never said I'm too busy, I just forgot! please stop being so busy, get off the cell phones, get off the computer. Stop. Take a moment and say I Love You! Mom. Would you like to take a walk in the park or just sit and talk. It doesn't cost you anything to call or visit, with a kind word or a hug. Let's say or do something. Your choice but do something memorable, with the one who means something to you. Recognize love when it's right in front of you!

Recognize

Loving Me first

I've always heard loving you first. Is

self preservation is the first law of nature.

Take care of me first, then I can help take care
of others... how about you? Just sayin...

HEALING HANDS

Thank you father, for giving me the patients, to come to work,with a gentle smile, healing hands to help. To be able to help others. Jesus walk with me. Give me the right words to say to encourage someone with a broken spirit, that awaits on my return to use my strength to help when they know longer have the willpower or strength to stand or walk. Father give me healing hands to touch someone and a gentle way. To give comfort and compassion to their ailing bodies, I ask this and

Jesus name.

amen

Hush Your Mouth

We need to be careful of what we say. What you say, can and will be harmful. We need to understand what it means, to say things out of our mouth, that's not cool. Like using profanity. We should not say certain things, because our life is being recorded just like everything else in this world. It's not what I'm saying... it's what the bible tells us. we just need to read and pay attention, and listen to what is the right things to say...I'm just saying, it's very easy to get caught up and before you know it "Bam!" we have said some slick stuff out of our mouth, it's hard to say the right things, all the time. It's very hard, but like they say nothing comes easy in this world. For most of us. We do have rules to follow, they are called the ten commandments.

The bible says, God said so. Just sayin..

{matthew 12:36}

INSPIRATIONAL WORDS

Just saying'... Is my way of writing inspirational words to teenagers, and young adults. Who may be interested, in reading inspiring words, for a broken heart, or whatever you may be facing and life. Almighty God, will always make away for you. Prayer is the key, Just talk to him. He has help me so many times. I can not count, the times he has saved my life. The most high is there, for you as well.

Just saying...

TODAY TOMORROW AND ALWAYS

People, change how they think and do things in life all the time.
Sometimes just to try and fit in. Teenagers try, at times to be someone
they are not, may be with a bad attitude, mood swings, maybe some
sort of a hardship has happen. Whatever life may have thrown at you.
You have to understand, life mishaps, happens to us all. What can you
do? or what do you need to do? try this say a little prayer or whisper
Jesus name, to redirect your mind, God, will always be with us because
he lives within us all. You do not try to be someone you are not.

Our Father, is in heaven and he always stay the same.
Today tomorrow and always. Trust his word, His promise
is true he can not lie. Jesus, loves us unconditionally, his
ways of thinking, is not our way of thinking."

I'm Just sayin...

BIBLE VERSES

Delight yourself in the Lord and he

will give you the desires of your heart

Psalm 37:4

I have many friends that I treat well. I do not tell
my secrets. Because when we are no longer

friends, out to the world my secrets goes...Just sayin

PRAY WITH RESPECT

Give God, the respect he deserves. He died on the cross for our sins. So we can have everlasting life, respect the power of prayer. We can not live and do whatever we want. That's not pleasing to God. Pray with respect. Be obedient, at least try, ask king Jesus to help you with all your problems.

Have faith give your life over to God.

Jesus got you, Do you got him?

He got You!

just sayin'...

PRAYING

Let me say this, we all know it does not cost you anything to pray.
But this is the way king Jesus tells us all to pray. To communicate,
tell him how you feel, and what need, not so much what you
want. Even though God already knows everything about us all.
God is our creator. He still want us all to pray and believe. Let's
acknowledge him and give thanks. It cost you nothing it's free.'

Just saying...

THE FAVOR

Only God, can give you favor. He can make a way out of know way. Jesus, can fill your life full of faith, if you only believe and him. Surrender yourself, Jesus loves you! your good health, is favor, everything we have, comes from God. Only the king can give you peace with favor, all we have is right now. Almighty God, promise this! Whenever we see a rainbow, it's a reminder to let us know Jesus, will be back one day. The gifts of favor. I'm just sayin...

Stop Look and Listen...

God is closer than you, may believe he is. God, says he will always be with you,. He lives within each and every one of us. If we only believe and trust his word God, so loved the world that he gave his only begotten son,that whosoever believeth in him should not perish But have everlasting life. Just sayin

Just Sayin'...

You know. I would have spared myself the pain, and grief of knowing things that was not meant for me to know. I would have saved myself the heartaches of love, if only I knew, it was not meant for me to know. Sometimes it's better not to know, certain things. That could break your heart. Somethings, are never, meant for you, to know. So you do not carry the pain of heartaches pertaining to love. With that being said don't be noisy Just sayin'....

WE ALL NEED JESUS

Heavenly Father,

we come to you in prayer. To say thank you! for loving us. Thank
you for waking us up, each and every morning. Giving us the
strength and guidance, we all so Desperately need. Father, we
come to you to ask you to continue, to watch over all of us. Our
families, and our friends. keep us all safe and Jesus name I pray...

Amen, the word amen! amen!! means something when we pray
it's important to say it, it's a closer, it's the final word to our prayer
before it travels to our heavenly father's ears. Just sayin...

Messages Of Love

★ Love is God
★ Love is respect for each other
★ Love is being in love
★ Love is tears of joy
★ Love is so deep it never dies
★ Love is so powerful
★ Love is true
★ Love is so real
★ Love is peace
★ Love is forever
★ Love is family
★ Love is a feeling
★ Love is a gift from heaven
★ Love has no words to explain
★ Love is Jesus he died for you and I.

FATHER

Father I come to you and prayer, I'm in need of a financial blessing father, only you can lift this burden from my life. I don't feel I have the strength or the energy to stand on my own. Your mercy and grace I need. Only you Jesus, can make me a stronger and a better person. Father I ask for forgiveness if I did or said anything to hurt anyone it wasn't intentionally. uplift my spirit, and set me free of debt. And Jesus name I pray.

Amen

YOUR SMILE

When you smile, I smile back. Your smile is so warm and inviting.
So contagious I must say. Your smile is medication to my heart. Your
smile brings joy to my life. Having you in my life brings me so much
happiness, so many precious memories, of yesteryears. When I hear your
voice, it makes my eyes sparkle, and my body dance. It just reminds
me of your smile, and you know when you smile. I smile back!

Just sayin...

THE BEST LIFE EVER

There is always a way out of any situation, If for any reason you feel lonely or depressed, Just remind yourself God is on the throne, You know you are so blessed, to be loved by our heavenly father. This is the best gift ever! It's called "life" given to the human race. To actually have someone to love you so much that he would die for us all. Not only one race, but all humanity. Jesus only asked of us to have faith and believe in him. He will not make or force you to love him.

God is awesome and there is nothing that's impossible for God to do. When you feel you are lost or in troubled. You need grace and mercy. You want God, to fight your battles, call on the King! His angels will. Try the King. He is there with open arms. Just pray and keep praying. Don't just stop praying after one or two times and then give up on Jesus. There is power in prayer. God is watching and listening. He is always on time. His time is not our time. "Try God" I'm just sayin...

STAY IN FAITH

We all have challenges, in this world. God, at times put us through a test. To test your faith sometimes, we think Jesus Christ, has abandon us he has not! we pray for what we want. We also want what God has just for us, right? staying in faith, sharing our knowledge of our heavenly father. This shows one another we have the faith without, seeing Jesus physically, we know that he does exist in each one of our hearts because we can feel him close by us. The bible tells us if we have a mustard seed, of faith the living God, has something to work with, within us. Our father works miracles each and every day! he gives us a gift everyday we wake up, the gift he gives to us all, Is a gift of life. We must stay in faith while God, rebuilds our faith. Our hopes and dreams, put your trust in Jesus, he will restore your faith, You will be transform and you will walk in faith.

The king can rebuild, he can do all things, if you only believe in him, Jesus, ways are not our ways not man made ways. You have to go through something in life to gain wisdom in life… praise the Lord at all times not only in church but you praise God, for all he has done for you! at any time. Now you have a testimony to share, Jesus wants you to share what you've learned with others, remember when two people are gathered together. God is in the midst, your best days are right now. Do not wait to get to know your true father, because no one is promised tomorrow

I praise Jesus know matter what!

This is my message to you

Mrs. Zina

LET'S BE HAPPY

We chose to sleep in anger instead of in each other's arms. You and I. We chose, each other for better or for worse. We supposed to have loved each other, and walked together, in life and started a new beginning. Instead, we chose to leave and take a different path. Until death due us part. We chose to fight instead of making love, we both let night fall, with a frown upon our face. Instead of making up. We chose to be miserable in darkness, before the twilight of dawn. While the stars were shining so bright before the sunrise, we still had anger in our hearts.We chose to have a free spirited husband and wife. We chose this, you and I. We chose to live in peace. We chose to love each other apart. Now we soar like two, Doves. Free. We chose this you and I.

just sayin'...

I've Been Loving You So...

You never knew. If you only knew, I've been
loving you so long. Secretly in my mind.

I must say, your love lives... in my heart, everyday and night, I
never knew I would ever feel this alive again. You came to restore
my broken heart, you lifted me up to a new height, I never thought
I could feel this way, so vibrant, so refresh. I'm so excited!

I feel like I'm six feet tall. When I only stand five feet.

To have you, to touch me. And kiss me, love me, where I miss
you. With your gentle touch... It's only in my mind, I know. I've
been loving you a little too long, a little too much, I need Jesus.

Just sayin'...

MY LITTLE ONE

My little one, so sweet so lovable.
I love you so. My heart melts when you look at me.
With a smile that is so unforgettable
God blessed me with you my little one.
I will always pray, God will continue to bless you and me. I'm always here
to take care of you my little one.
Hands so tiny, feet so small, you smell so sweet
all bundle up just for me. God knew exactly
what I needed when he gave me you.

My little one

Printed in the United States
By Bookmasters